I'm really not a

But... Can I shov

way to do that?

This book belongs to:

____

Made in the USA
Lexington, KY
19 December 2019

58862349R00068